PIG FACE
COLORING BOOK

CRYSTAL
COLORING BOOKS

ISBN-13: 978-1979768276
ISBN-10: 1979768277

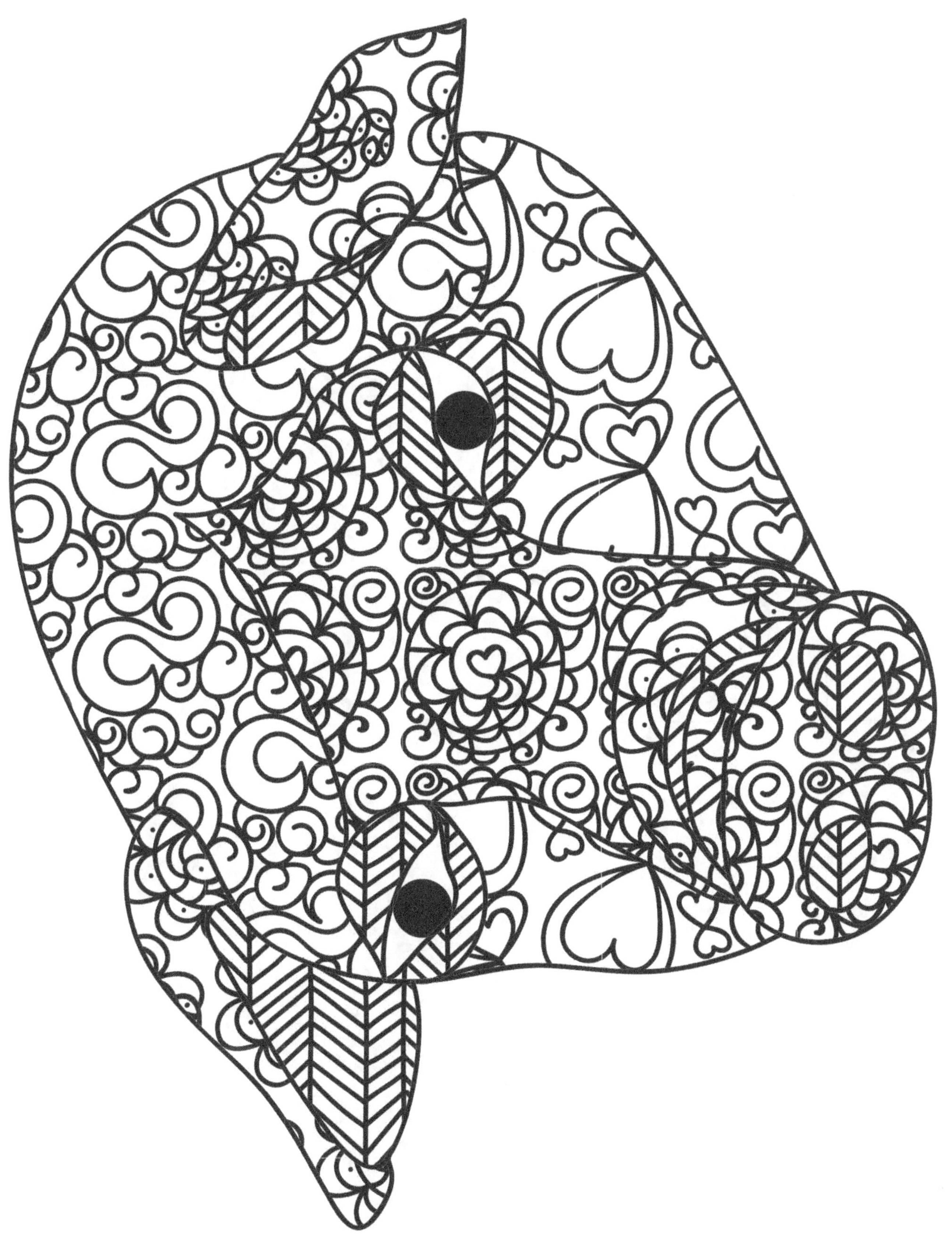

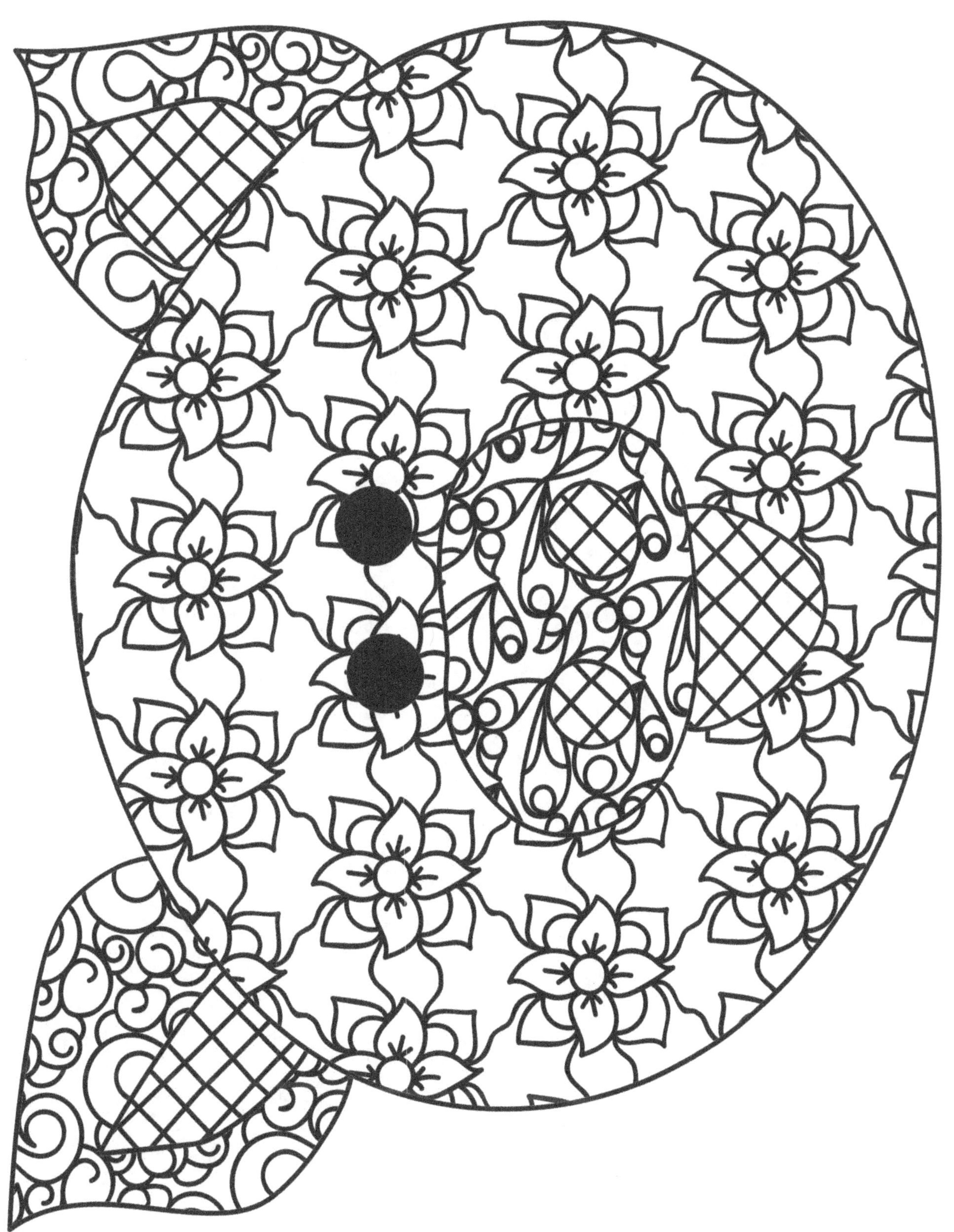

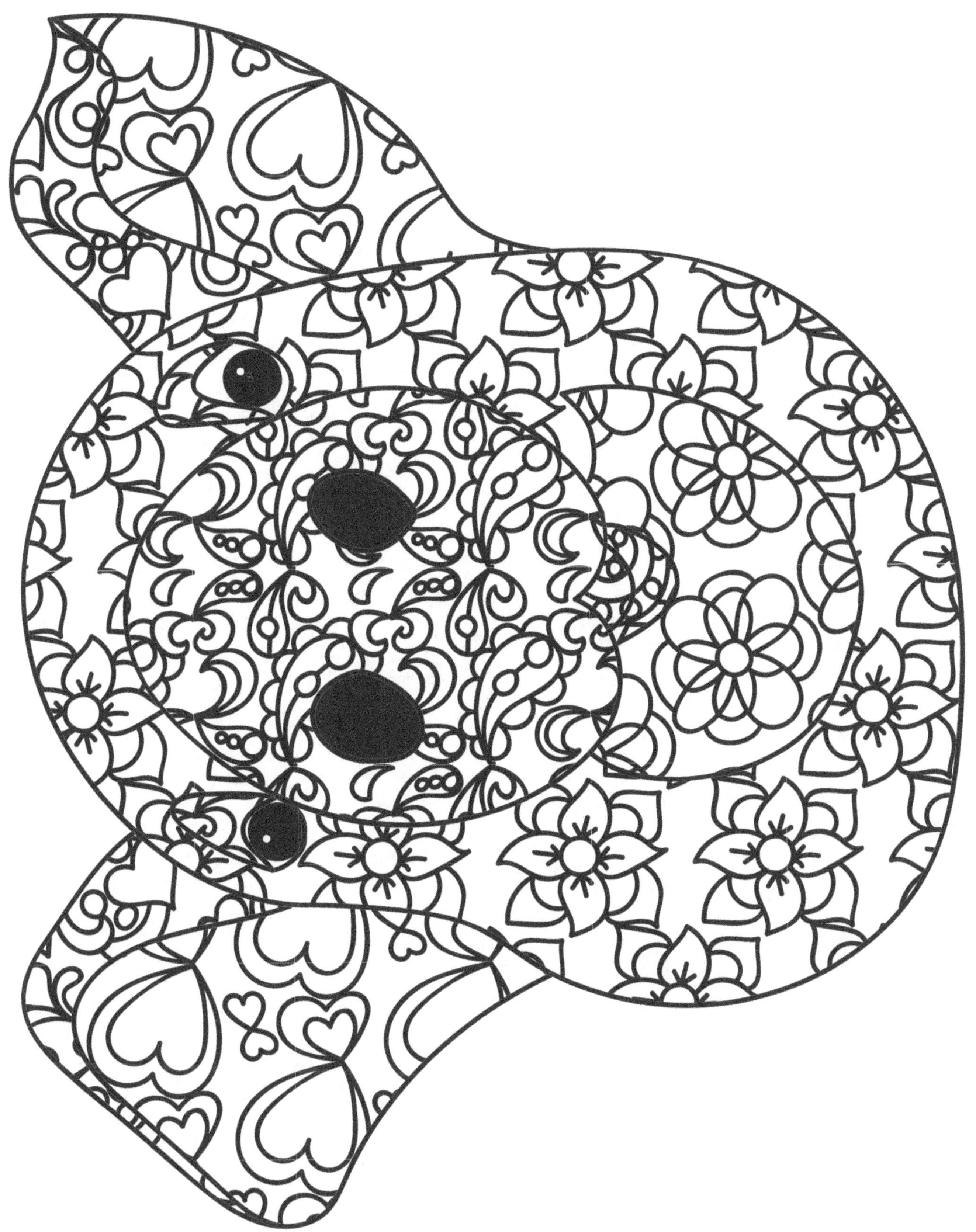

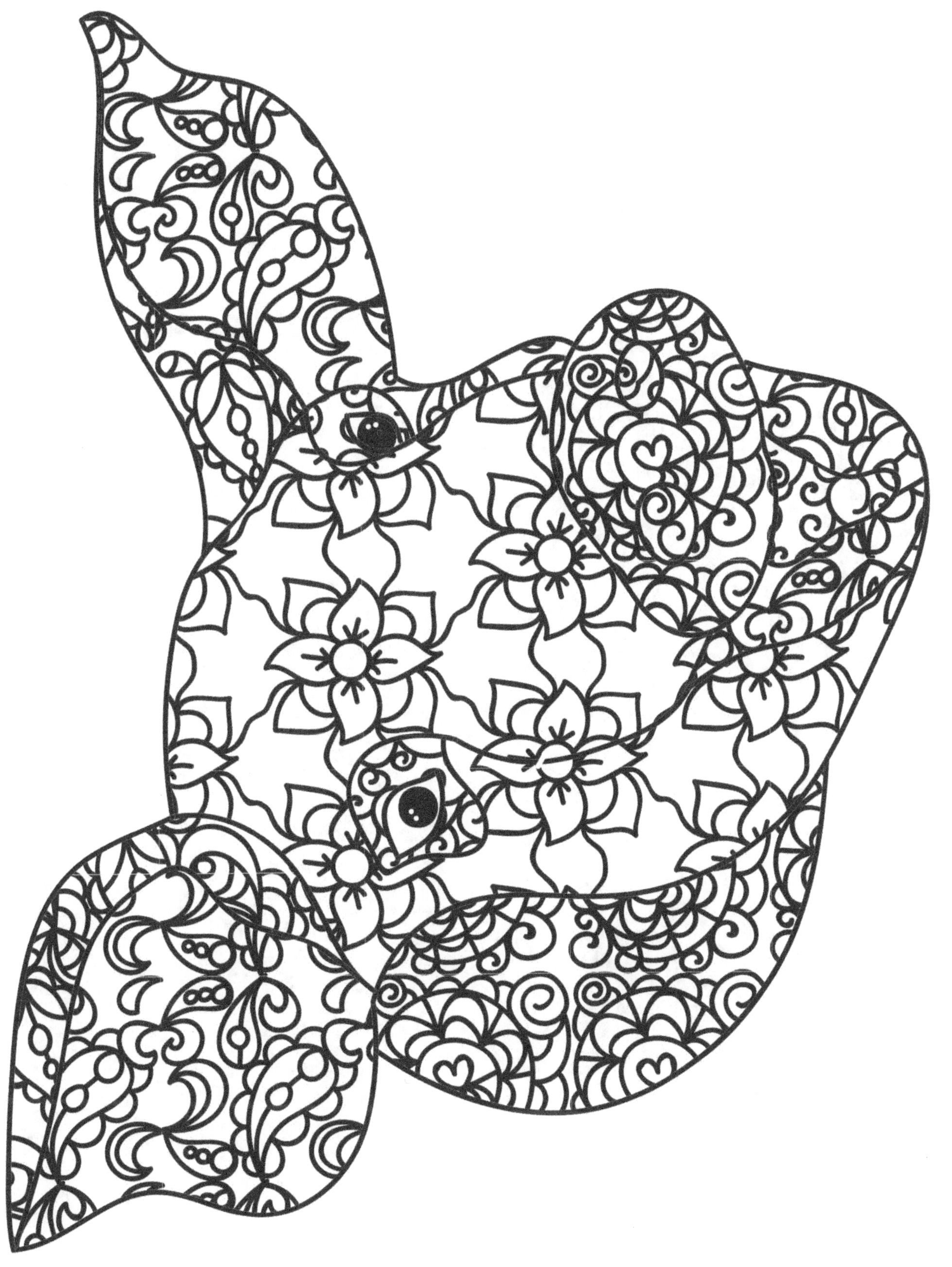

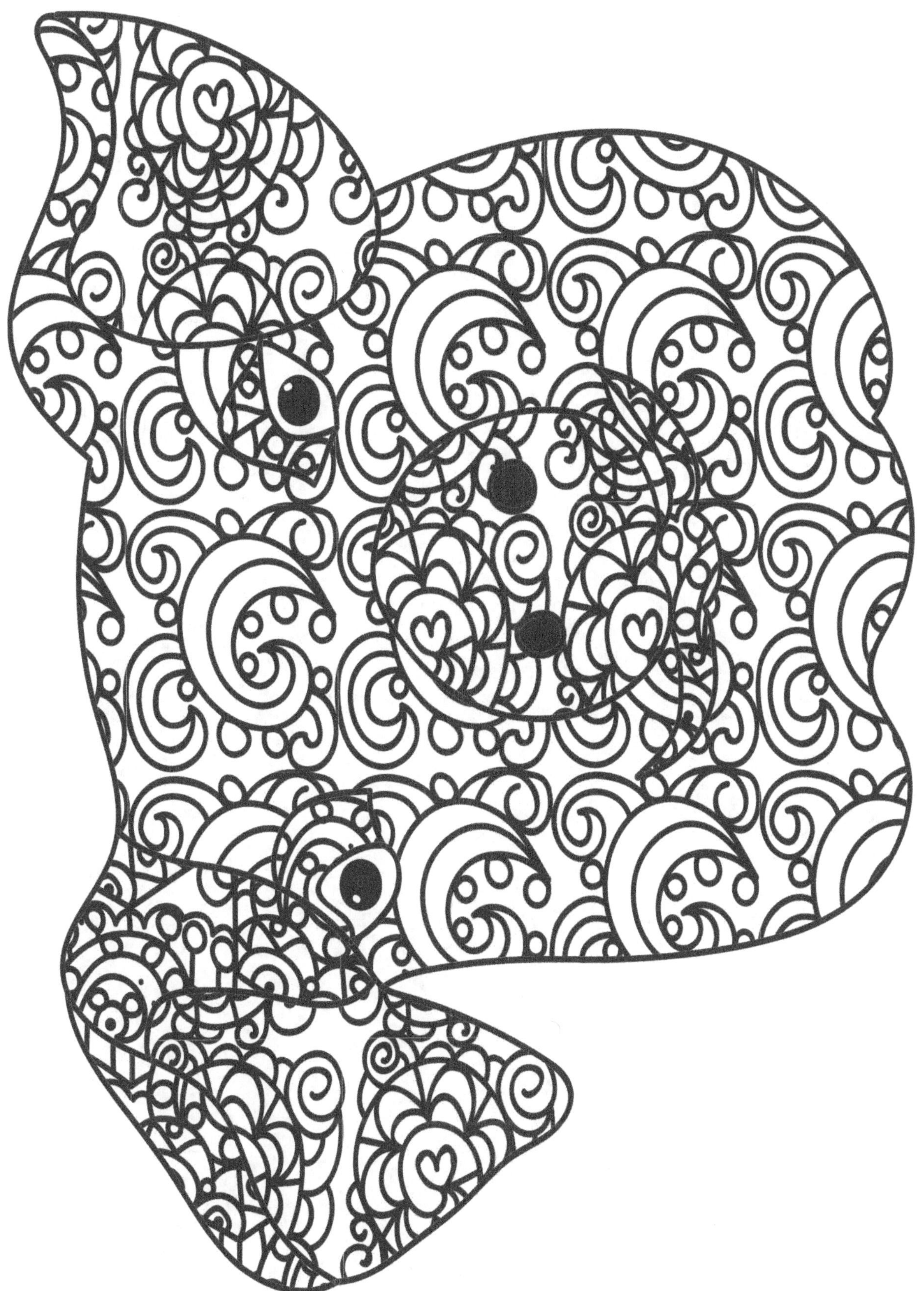

COLOR TEST PAGE

COLOR TEST PAGE